MW01601651

ISBN: 979-8-9898049-2-4

First Printing Edition 2024

Unless otherwise indicated, Scripture quotations are taken from the New International Version or New Living Translation of the bible.

Published by One Source For Resources

About the Author

Demonay has been married to Franklin Moss for 8 years. They are a blended family with two older boys. Together they have 6yr, 5yr, 3 yr and 8 month old. They live in Florida.

Demonay was led by the Lord to create this devo and to create these two Facebook platforms to help people.

Sticky Bible Study was established in 2013 on Facebook. This platform is designed to help people grow closer to God.

Changebydee was established in 2020. This a platform to help people learn and become debt-free through Godly principles.

Thank you so much for choosing this devo!

TABLE OF CONTENTS

INTRODUCTION

This is Volume 2 of Rooted Faith Walk: SEEK devotional, it's based on our true story from July 2023-November 2023. God told us to move to Florida. We had to sell the stuff in our Texas house to get to Florida. We were BROKE and in over 120,000 in DEBT. We are a blended family of 6/8, depending on the season. We thrive in worship and seeking God's presence. As of now, we paid off 20,000. Spending time with God is the first thing that every person in our house does before anything else. It's a standard in our home.
We encourage you to try it.

God has called us to share our testimony with the world so that more people can believe, strength their faith, and choose to follow God.

How to Interact With this Book:
Each day provides a daily daytime devotional and a night response. The night response should be read during the day so you can have time to complete the night response based on the act of kindness you did for that day. Use your devotional, first thing when you wake up and around dinner time. Try to be in a less noisy area so God can really speak to you. I sit at the dinner table in the mornings and after I clean the kitchen from dinner I sit in quiet room. Try not to read in a lying down position because you might fall asleep or not retain what you've read. Always have your bible and a notepad in case you need more room to added notes.

 Soak  Sketch  Seek

This Book of the Law shall not depart from your mouth, but you shall meditate on it day and night, so that you may be careful to do according to all that is written in it. For then you will make your way prosperous, and then you will have good success. Joshua 1:8

DW

2

It's Rest Day!

Materials you may need
- Bible
- Pen/Pencil
- Blank Paper
- Sticky Notes

Use your Pencil.
Pull out your schedule.

When can you spend time with God this season in DAY and at NIGHT? Fill in each sticky note or create your own.

Post your stickies where you can remember to look.

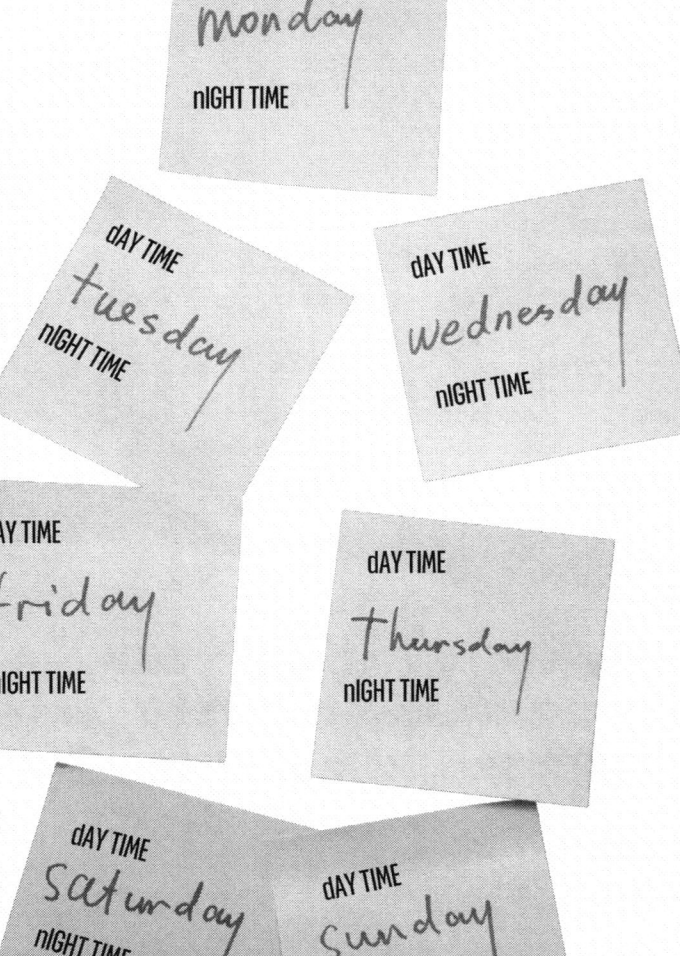

FAVOR OF GOD

CHAPTER 1

Encouragement

Doing things a certain way, you will experience the favor of God. -Moss Family

If you want favor with both God and man, and a reputation for good judgment and common sense, then trust the Lord completely; don't ever trust yourself. 6 In everything you do, put God first, and he will direct you and crown your efforts with success. Proverbs 3:4-5

LENDER

During this season, I would do the budget and realize I didn't have enough money for gas and food. We managed to pay monthly debt bills and home bills monthly. So I would ask God what to do. Well in November 2022, God told us, "I know you are short on maintaining y 'all's bills right now, but after paying your bills, with any extra money you receive, place it on debt, and I will handle gas and food." So, we did, even using our entire income tax refund (9,000) to pay off that Discover Credit Card. It was incredible how blessings were coming from left to right as we sought God daily and continued to obey, regardless of the amount we received.

1. Growing up, which mentality did your gradians instill in you- that of a borrower or a lender?

2. Personal Reflection: As a maturing adult, would you describe yourself as a borrower or lender?

3.* Find another scripture in the Bible that discusses being a borrower or a lender, and write about which one you want to be?

NIGHT 1  # Seek

chose a way to serve someone today

Reflect:

Serve Ideas
Meditate on 1 Peter 4:10-11
Create sandwiches, go pass them out
Go out and serve someone other than yourself
Pay for someone's meal
Go on a lunch date with a friend and buy their meal

BLINDED

February 2023, We both looked at each other and said, "We are moving to Florida." Confirmation was coming from everywhere. We let days pass, knowing we had a total of 30 days to move out. One day, our bedroom flooded, the A/C went out, and a raccoon died on the side of the roof of the house. Within these 30 days, it became clear that it was beyond time to go. Additionally, God told us that we couldn't rent an apartment for 6 months and then move to Florida later; instead, we had to move in with a married couple and their children in Texas until I give birth to sweet Brooklynn. God's word was, "You will not get the glory out of this." Mind y'all, we are extremely broke, so we are having a hard time seeing how we are getting to Florida and providing for our children.

1. Have you ever been asked to do something, but then you didn't know how you would do it, yet you agreed anyway? Explain.

2. *What does it mean in your life to walk by Faith?

3. Do you believe that God goes with you to overcome any obstacle you face each day? Explain

---

NIGHT 2  **Seek**

share @ sticky bible study

Reflect:

<u>**Memory verse: Isaiah 26:3**</u>
- Create a index card with this scripture.
- Carry this scripture with you for this week.
- Recite this scripture twice a day minimum.

ENDURANCE

And we know that for those who love God all things work together for good,[a] for those who are called according to his purpose. Romans 8:28

March 2023: I kid you not, we are down to the wire. We have 3 days left in our house. At around 8 pm, we received a phone call from friends at our Church (Gateway Houston in Katy). They mentioned that for the last 3 days, we had been on their minds. They suggested checking with God but believed we should move in with them from March 28 until the baby comes. We prayed, and we agreed. We moved in with them; they have 5 children and 3 dogs. This family was a great example of what it looked like to follow God. We learned so much from them. We transitioned to Florida. We stayed in hotels for 21 days. All 6 of us in one room with each other. Trusting God's promise as we waited.

1. List everything that is troubling you.

2. *Do you believe God has a plan for your good? Why do you believe that?

3. Talk with your accountability partner today; ask your partner how you can pray for them. Listen to them, and when they are finished, pray for them immediately. Jot down what you prayed for.

share @ sticky bible study

NIGHT 3  **Seek**

Reflect:

Worship for 30 mins
Turn on worship music
Display lyrics on the screen
Sing out loud and focus on God
Eliminate distractions

STANDARDS

So let's not sleepwalk through life like those others. Let's keep our eyes open and be smart. 1 Thess.5:6

June 2023-July 2023: We stayed with the McCoys for 1 month in Florida. This week, I have been asking God for the vision of our next steps. At the McCoy's House, at 3:33 am in July 2023, the Lord woke me up out of my sleep and said, "We will purchase a home."

---

1. Read 1 Samuel 3. Why do you believe Samuel kept going to Eli?

2. *When I am woken up in the middle of the night, I usually pray as I walk through the house, checking children and interior doors. What do you typically do?

3. Read **2 Corinthians 10:2-5** create T chart. What are two types of standards in this world? Which one do you and your household live by?

share @ sticky bible study

NIGHT 4  # Seek

Reflect:

<u>Sermon</u>
watch an online sermon.(pick wisely)
watch one of your pastor's sermons.
take notes
what is one take away you learned

DETERMINED

"The wicked flee when no one pursues, but the righteous are bold as a lion." Proverbs 28:1

> The next day, I started the prequalification process for the home while still staying at McCroy's house. I planned to use my previous job's income along with my husband's income to qualify for a house. However, it did not work because we switched careers, so we had to wait for 6 months.

1. Have you ever heard a word from God and acted on it immediately, only to not get the response you expected? Tell me about it below.

2. *What promises has God given you? If you don't know, it's okay. STOP and pray (say: God, what promise do you have for me?).

3. . What do you need prayer for? Call your accountability partner and pray with each other.

share @ sticky bible study

NIGHT 5  # Seek

Reflect:

Meditate
Deuteronomy 28
Genesis 22
1 King 17

RIGHTEOUS

DAY 6

Surely, LORD, you bless the righteous; you surround them with your favor as with a shield. Psalm 5:12

> I started the prequalification process and met Gene (Realtor). He helped me connect with the middle school principal, and I got hired even though my degree was pending. I was so excited. I am now a 6th-grade teacher in Ruskin. Everything was finalized two days before teachers returned to school (August 2, 2023). Childcare has not been finalized yet, so I am still trying to figure out all the kinks.

1. While the Lord shields you, he provides _____.

2. *Why do you think the LORD has to shield you?

3. Write down a goal or goals you have for yourself to complete within the next three weeks.

NIGHT 6

 **Seek**

Reflect:

Goals

Jot down your goals.
Find scriptures that will help you
Achieve your goals
Recite your goals (minimum of two Times a day)

Rest Day

Over this past week, reflect, how has God spoken to you? What's one thing your going to change?

....

....

....

....

....

....

....

....

....

....

....

....

....

....

....

....

FEAR OF GOD

CHAPTER 2

Encouragement

Doing things a certain way, you fear God.

-Moss Family

God is your constant source of stability; he abundantly provides safety and great wisdom; he gives all this to those who fear him.
Isaiah 33:6

REST

DAY 8

Jesus says "Come to me, all of you who are weary and burdened, and I will give you rest."
Matthew 11:28 (CSB)

How was last week rest day? Did you enjoy it? Taking a day of rest each week is well needed. Rest for me is spending time with God, with the kids and with hubby, and laying everything at the feet of Jesus.

1. What happens when things get crazy in your world? Do you rest or try to keep up with it all on your own?

2. *With how crazy this world is now a lot of your time is consumed. When you do rest, how do you spend your time for that day? How often do you get to rest?

3 . Who is responsible for carrying your weary (burnout) and burdens (sufferings)?

NIGHT 8  **Seek**
Reflect:

Memory verse: Exodus 33:12-14
- Create a index card with this scripture.
- Carry this scripture with you for this week.
- Recite this scripture twice a day minimum.

PRAY

"But they who wait for the Lord shall renew their strength; they shall mount up with wings like eagles; they shall run and not be weary; they shall walk and not faint." Isaiah 40:31

I took time to seek God. I heard nothing. So I waited and went to look for daycares. Erica, a family from **Series 1 (Soak)** has a childcare service so they kept the children the first week of school for $490. They were located an hour a way from the Ruskin Job, heading past Fish Hawk. **Thank goodness they kept all 4 children.** This gave me more time to find them childcare. Childcare for 3 children was 650-750 a week. All three children would be at different daycares. Or I could have put 2 children in one elementary, 1 child in another elementary, and put the new born in house daycare only paying $225 a week. But with us living 1 hour away plus drop off I would have to get up by 4 am to make sure I am on time as a middle school teacher.

1. In your waiting, do you sit still or do you keep worrying?

2. *When you worry, what does God want us to do? Psalm 46:10 Philippians 4:6-7

3. Call your accountability partner. Listen to them. Ask them for prayer. Tell them yours. y'all pray. Jot down topics below and put today's date

---

NIGHT 9  ## Seek

Reflect:

Prayer
Who in your life needs prayer
Pray for others
Write a prayer out for 3 people

CONSTANT

God is your constant source of stability; he abundantly provides safety and great wisdom; he gives all this to those who fear him. Isaiah 33:6

So I went to training week 1. I was up at 4 am, getting everyone dressed and dropping everyone off. I made it to work by 8:30 am (I was 30 minutes late each day). I worked hard to put two children in Head Start, but they had orientation at the same time I was supposed to be at work. I ran all over. I am trying to understand why I can't find childcare for my infant. In Riverview, childcare was super expensive, but it wasn't available for all three children to be at the same daycare. Meanwhile, blessings are flowing in. We are still seeking God day and night. We are still paying towards our debt.

1. Based on the scripture above, what does God provide? Who is God?

2. *When things are constantly pulling you from left to right, what do you do to remain calm?

3. Today, I will share with someone new! Tell them how you were reminded that God is your constant source of stability.

NIGHT 10      # Seek

Reflect:

Worship for 30 min
Turn on worship music.
Display the words/lyrics on the screen. Sing out loud.
Focus on God eliminate distractions

BETWEEN

The Lord himself goes before you and will be with you; he will never leave you nor forsake you. Do not be afraid; do not be discouraged." Deuteronomy 31:8

I had the keys, and I arrived in my classroom. I walked in, and it suddenly hit me: I have nothing to put in this classroom. I had given everything I once had for a classroom away to many, many people. So, I sat and cried—weeping of joy, also of sadness. I know God is able to do immeasurably more than I can think or imagine, but I couldn't see it. I called my hubby, and he encouraged me. I went to training. At the end of training, they had an ABUNDANCE of supplies, on a first-come, first-serve basis. I cried more and more. I prayed and gave God the glory.

1. Have you ever given things away that you love? Were you being generous or obedient or both? What was it?

2. *What does this picture mean to you??

But I love it, God

Give me what you love.

3. Read John 10:10. What's the difference between the thief's and Jesus' purpose on earth?

NIGHT 11  # Seek

Reflect:

Prayer
Who in your life needs prayer?
Pray for others.
Write a prayer out for 3 people.
Pray for yourself

ABUNDANCE

I will make you into a great nation, and I will bless you; I will make your name great, and you will be a blessing. I will bless those who bless you, and whoever curses you I will curse; and all peoples on earth will be blessed through you Genesis 12:1-3

A friend I met from Love First Church during Art of Marriage (Katrina)(Online) called me. She said, "Hey, my mom just called and told me that she has extra supplies. You have to drive to Tampa, but do you want them?" I said YES! When we arrived, this Church had school supplies and clothes. All six of us in my family left with something. Praise God. God showed up again!

1. What is a blessing?

2. *What is God saying to me and to you?

3. How do you think I feel about God and my classroom now?

NIGHT 12      # Seek

Reflect:

Serve ideas
Go volunteer and help the elderly
Go volunteer at Boys and Girls club near you
Volunteer at a shelter
Help out at a food pantry

DISTRAUGHT

For I know the plans I have for you," declares the Lord, "plans to prosper you and not to harm you, plans to give you hope and a future. Jeremiah 29:11

But now, I have become so distraught. We are being asked to move out of McCoy's house in two days. My job is right by his house, and my husband is already driving 2 hours both ways each day. So, we decided to relocate in the middle of both jobs. We don't know how or what or when, but we looked into hotels because we know we have to purchase a home in less than 6 months.

1.*Genesis 37:23-28, Joseph's brothers were upset about a vision Joseph had, so they decided to ___. Which chapter in scripture talks about the vision God gave Joseph?

2. Genesis 45:1-4: Did Joseph have stability? Was he respected? How were his brothers when they realized it was him?

3. After reading Romans 8:28, what did you learn about God's ability? (Fill in the blank) God can _____ regardless .

NIGHT 13  # Seek
Reflect:

Meditate
Philippians 4:4
Romans 12:12
Psalm 21:5-7

Rest Day

Over this past week, reflect, how has God spoken to you? What's one thing your going to change?

....

....

....

....

....

....

....

....

....

....

....

....

....

....

ACKNOWLEDGE GOD

CHAPTER 3

Encouragement

Doing things a certain way, you acknowledge God. -Moss Family

Trust in the Lord with all your heart, and do not lean on your own understanding. In all your ways acknowledge him, and he will make straight your paths. Proverbs 3:5-6

DIRECTION

We prayed and asked God for direction. My little brother Silas informed us about an app months ago, designed for people traveling around the world. We used my Houston income to help us qualify for this program (thank goodness we left McCoy's house before my Houston job ended). We relocated to Bradenton with this app, which is 30 minutes away from my husband's job. We couldn't move to Sarasota location because they didn't have any homes available.

1. Have you ever wondered why things played out the way they did? What happened?

2. Have you reached the other side of it and reflected back on the way things used to be and how they are now? Stop and give God the glory.

3. *Hebrews 11:1-2: What does it mean to walk by Faith and not by sight?

Night 15  Seek

Reflect:

Memory verse: Proverbs 22
- Select a verse from this chapter
- Create a index card with this scripture.
- Carry this scripture with you for this week.
- Recite this scripture twice a day minimum.

COMMUNITY

"Ask and it will be given to you; seek and you will find; knock and the door will be opened to you. For everyone who asks receives; the one who seeks finds; and to the one who knocks, the door will be opened. Matthew 7: 7-8

September 2023, still standing on God's promise. In November 2022, in Series 1 Soak, remember that God told us to pay off our debt and that He would provide gas and food. Last night, I debated whether to go to Church or use the little gas I had left to get the kids to school tomorrow. I decided to go to Church. We went to Church. Towards the end of the Community Group, they asked for prayer requests, and I raised my hand, asking for provision and healing. I said "I need prayer for my back to be healed, gas in my car, a ticket to the upcoming women's conference that's in 3 days, and money to start a business". Everyone prayed for me. Afterwards, I received a ticket to the women's conference because the daughter of the person in charge of the concerts was in the room. I received a full tank of gas in my vehicle. My back pain was released. Someone else gave me $20 (I was told by God to save this for gas). I gave thanks to God for providing yet again.

1.*God sees you; He wants you in a community group each semester they offer it at your Church. Virtual Church is not your only means of connecting. How are you going to improve this semester in your community groups?

2. If I had not opened my mouth for prayer, how do you think I would have received gas to make it back home, etc.? Or do you think I should have just stayed home and not gone at all because I didn't have gas money?

3. When you need help, who do you ask? Do you believe that there are people that have different perspectives than you in this world?

Night 16  # Seek

Reflect:

Sermon
Watch an online sermon.(pick wisely)
Rewatch one of your pastor's sermons.
Take notes
What is one take away you learned?

CHILDREN

August 2023, still standing on God's promise. In November 2022, in Series 1 Soak, remember that God told us to pay off our debt and that He would provide gas and food. We dropped Lydia off at school. We had 11 miles to empty. We parked at a gas station. We asked, "Hey, can you help us with gas?" They said yes. They gave us $3. I just sat in the car and kept waiting. Elizabeth said, "Mom, let's go get gas, God blessed us." I didn't realize God had blessed us because I was expecting to fill the gas tank up. But we put the $3 in the gas tank, and it went from 11 miles to 31 miles. We were able to make it home. Praise God for providing.

1. Read Matthew 18: 1-11, How does Jesus feel about the children?

2. Read Luke 16:10, How does Jesus feel about being faithful?

3.* Reflect back on this past week, how has God blessed you or the people around you and you didn't realize it right away?

Night 17  # Seek

Reflect: How did you help the world around you?

Serve Ideas
Go collect trash from an outside area
Pass out waters to those in need
Help someone complete their project

HEALING

Day 18

Is anyone among you sick? Let them call the elders of the church to pray over them and anoint them with oil in the name of the Lord. And the prayer offered in faith will make the sick person well; the Lord will raise them up. If they have sinned, they will be forgiven. James 5: 14-15 (NIV)

July 2023, Still standing on God's promise. November 2022 in Series 1 Soak, remember God told us to pay off debt and he will provide gas and food. We drove all the way until the gas tank said 0 miles. We were driving on the freeway and we made it JUST in time to closest gas station. We prayed over a woman who was having a hard time getting out of her car. Her knees where weak. We prayed for healing in her knees.

1. I went to the gas station for me, but in the midst, I helped _____.

2. Challenge: Even though you came to the store or worked, for yourself, Today, intentionally look for someone you can pray for. Share below when you come back home.

3. God wants us to confess our sins to each other and pray for each other so that _____? Read James 5:16.

Night 18  # Seek

Reflect:

Journaling
Create a list of the things your grateful for
Create a list of all the ways you have served others
Create a list of all the ways God has provided for you
Write about the person you helped today and tell how it
Made you feel

LIMITED

"Do not be anxious about anything, but in every situation, by prayer and petition, with thanksgiving, present your requests to God. And the peace of God, which transcends all understanding, will guard your hearts and your minds in Christ Jesus." phil 4:6-7

Jan 2023, Still standing on God's promise. In November 2022, in Series 1 Soak, remember that God told us to pay off debt, and He would provide gas and food. My sister met me at Kroger, handed me her card, and left. She told me to get the groceries we needed. No cap. I cried a dozen times. I couldn't wrap my mind around not having boundaries. I love budgets. God told me, "GET WHAT YOU NEED, DON'T LIMIT ME." I thought, I can use the WIC card for fruits and veggies. I thought, well, I don't have to get this or that. I thought, let me keep it at $50. I don't want to take advantage of my sister. I tried to spend only $50, but with groceries so high and nothing in our pantry or no toiletries, it was impossible. Then God said, "You will not get the glory from this; get what you need." I cried so much.

1. On YouTube, watch 2 out of 4 of these videos and answer this question: After watching, How would you describe God's Character?
   List of video titles below:
   - "Don't Limit what God can do for you, God Gifting Us by Demonay Moss
   - God gets the glory He is Faithful praise his name. by Demonay Moss.
   - I don't have it but God does by Demonay_Moss
   - Don't Limit God: God will provide food for your family by Demonay Moss

2. Draw conclusions about what God was doing to my heart

3. *Read Matthew 6:24-34 what should our minds be focused on instead of worrying?

Night 19  Seek
Reflect:

Prayer Walk
Listen to Genesis 24
get your water
go walk and pray 20min

SAMARITAN

Whoever shuts their ears to the cry of the poor will also cry out and not be answered. Proverbs 21:13

September 18, 2023, Today I realized that after Franklin left for work this morning, I didn't have my car keys. The girls were ready to go to school, but I was unsure how to manage without the keys. I remembered three people I could call who lived close by. So, I texted them and asked for help. The person who has a 1st grader and lives in the same complex was available to take them to school for me. Unfortunately, there wasn't enough room for Landon, Brooklynn, and me. I took a picture of her license plate, and she took a picture of them when they arrived at school. Once they were dropped off, she told me they are welcome to ride with her each morning. She sent me a picture of everything I needed to know. She was very loving and caring.

---

1. What does Samaritan mean? How would you explain this to someone new to the faith or someone that isn't saved yet?

2. Read Luke 10:25-37 What did you learn about the Samaritan?

3.*What would you have done if you saw this Samaritan?

Night 20  # Seek

Reflect:

Accountability

What habit and goal are you currently working on? Share it with your partner so they can hold you accountable!

Rest Day

Read Proverbs 22:6. Yourself, Future kids, your children, grandchildren, and or step children

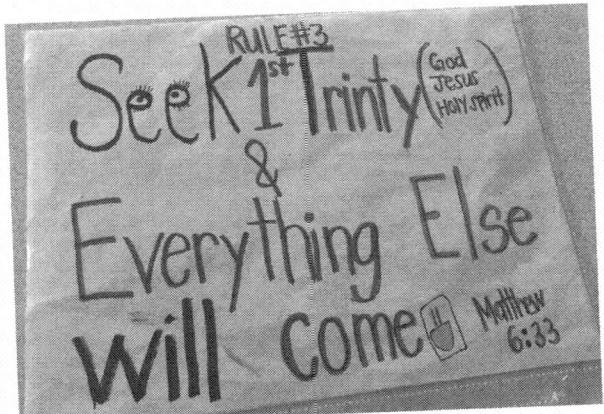

Read Scripture, find the scriptures you want to use daily to influence yourself. Create a visual to remind you of each verse. This tool helps you memorize scriptures.

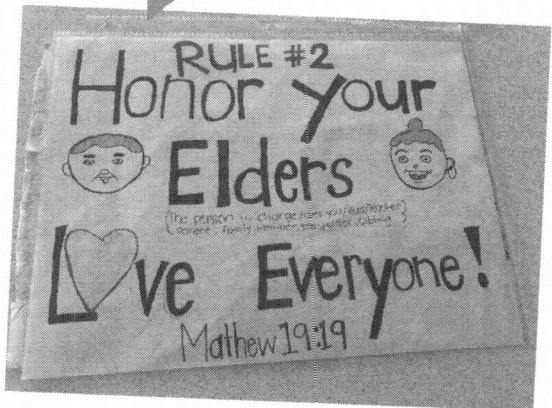

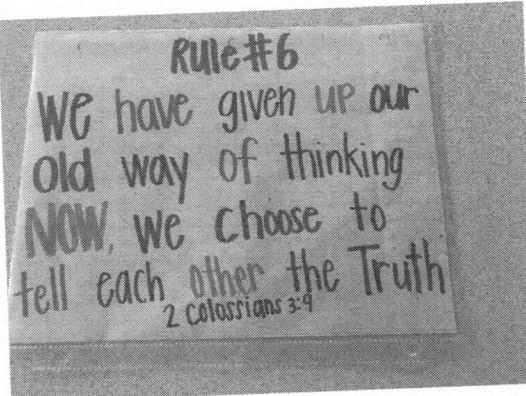

SAME GOD

CHAPTER 4

Encouragement
Doing things a certain way, experience the
same God. -Moss Family

Jesus Christ the same yesterday, and to
day, and for ever. Hebrew 13:8

BRADENTON

"The poor and needy search for water, but there is none; their tongues are parched with thirst. But I the Lord will answer them; I, the God of Israel, will not forsake them Isaiah 41:17

We relocated to a Bradenton Airbnb, much closer to my husband's job. Despite this, I continued looking for childcare in Ruskin and worked throughout the week. By Friday, I couldn't find childcare and ended up driving from 5:30 am until 6:30 pm, feeling restless. Franklin suggested I quit working and find a job in Bradenton due to the costly commute and lack of income.

1. Read Isaiah 40:28-31 NIV: Fill in the blanks:

2. What does the word "submit" mean?

_____those who _____ in the Lord

they willl _____ their strength.

They will _____on wings like _____;

3.*What do you do when you feel restless?

they will _____and _____ grow weary,

they will _____and _____be faint.

Night 22  Seek

Reflect:

<u>**Invite-Psalm 66:5-6**</u>
Go on a lunch date
Share this book with a friend!
(Bring extras copy or pay for their meal)

CHAOS

You will keep me in perfect peace as my mind remains focused on you because I trust in you. Isaiah 26:3

> Saturday became a day of REST. I immersed myself in God's presence, listening, praying, and reading His word. I still managed our living space and engaged with all four children, keeping my mind focused on God.

1. Although we face so much each day, there are scriptures designed for us to meditate on so we REMAIN even in chaos. Read Lamentations 3:22-23. What is God revealing to you?

2. Spend time with God today. Find a quiet space, even if it's your car. Listen. Obey. Say, "Lord, I am listening." Spend 30 minutes with him uninterrupted the best you can. If that means fasting for lunch to make it work, DO IT.

3. After reading question 2, spend time answering these questions: What does it mean to rest? Seek? How can you grow in the ways you spend time with God?

Night 23  # Seek

Reflect:

Meditate
Psalm 55 or 23
Find a quiet space
what is God revealing
Highlight what stands out

SAFETY

In peace I will lie down and sleep,
for you alone, LORD, make me dwell
in safety. Psalms 4:8

> This Airbnb was a one-bedroom, one-bath unit. An Airbnb is a home that isn't yours; someone else's furniture, pots, pans, dishes, towels, TVs, and Wi-Fi are in the home, and you pay a fee to borrow their space. My husband, four children, and I found a way to fit into that Queen bed each night. We also managed to ensure the house was cleaned every night, and we cooked as much as we could. God showed up for us..

1.Read Acts 27:25-36. How did God provide safety? What did they go through, and how long did they endure this storm?

2.Read Genesis 6:9-22. What did God tell Noah, and how was God going to keep him safe?

3.Pray for yourself:(fill in the blanks with what you need for today)
Lord, thank you for _____. God, you always _____.
I need _____. God, I release _____.
I want to be used by _____.
Help me believe you are my safety net again. Amen.

Night 24  **Seek**

Reflect:

Reflect
1. How has God shown up for you?
2. Praise his name
3. Create a thankful list

 CRY

A voice says, "Cry out." And I said, "What shall I cry?" "All people are like grass, and all their faithfulness is like the flowers of the field. 7 The grass withers and the flowers fall,   because the breath of the Lord blows on them. Surely the people are grass. 8 The grass withers and the flowers fall, but the word of our God endures forever." Isaiah 40:6-8

After experiencing that week, I cried out to God. I had a decision to make. I chose to submit to my spouse, and on our wedding anniversary, August 8, I quit that job.

1.Let's talk. What are some things on your mind? Are they weighing heavily on you? Pour out below. Be honest; it's just me.

2.Spend 10 minutes or more crying out to God.

3.Research these scriptures. Psalm 107:1–3, Psalm 103:2–5, Philippians 4:6–7, Psalm 95:2.

Night 25  **Seek**

Reflect:

<u>**Memory verse: Psalm 23:1**</u>
- Create a index card with this scripture.
- Carry this scripture with you for this week.
- Recite this scripture twice a day minimum.

BLIND

"God will lead the blind by ways they have not known, along unfamiliar paths I will guide them; I will turn the darkness into light before them and make the rough places smooth. These are the things I will do; I will not forsake them." (Isaiah 42:16 NIV)

Sunday has arrived. We've made a decision that we could not afford to drive 40 minutes for Church (Love First) since we were going Sundays and Wednesdays, so we needed to find something closer. We googled, and Bayside Community Church was super close. We went and checked it out. We loved it.

1. Based on Isaiah 42:16, who will lead you? Where will he lead you?

2. On YouTube, watch this video: God will lead the blind by Demonay Moss. What are you learning about God's character?

3. Do you believe that no matter which direction you take, because you belong to God, He will provide for you?

Night 26  # Seek

Reflect:

Journal/Draw
Grab a blank sheet of paper and a pen. Sit still for 15 minutes and let the Lord lead you on what to write, draw, or note.
When you're finished, go back and reflect. If you need to, you can take a picture of it, rip it up, or store it.
Either way, you have been released, and now you're ready to receive from God.

GENEROSITY

Day 27

Commit to the Lord whatever you do,
and he will establish your plans.
Proverbs 16:3

It's Monday, and I started off focusing on one person at a time. First was enrolling Lydia in school. I signed her up and learned about Purple Heart. The school helped with uniforms, backpacks, and the enrollment process was smooth. They told me to go check out the Dreamcenter because they offered FREE childcare for after school. I immediately broke down into tears. I cried with joy because, for the first time in Florida, I felt the weight lifted off my shoulders. If I have to work from 7 am to 5 pm, I know my girl will be taken care of.

1. When was the last time someone helped you, and you felt the weight lifted?

2. Today, intentionally help someone else besides yourself today. Journal it.

3. How did your generosity make you feel afterward?

Night 27  # Seek

Reflect:

Self Care
Take time with God your way
tonight!
Minimum 30min

Rest Day

USE WHAT YOU HAVE

You discern my going out and my lying down; you are familiar with all my ways. psalm139: 3

Sept 12, 2023 The Lord said USE WHAT YOU HAVE
update the titles, description, record, upload, and thumbnails on your Youtube page, use the hair that is in your drawer to do your own hair, write your book based on your real life experiences, post on Changebydee, post on Sticky Bible Study, sell stuff on marketplace, coach people on how to budget, coach other parents on how to structure routine for their home. God reminded me of widow and oil (2 King 4)

Study---2 Kings 4:1-7, John 6:1-14, and 1 Peter 4:10-11

How can you use what you have to improve the situation around you?

TRUST GOD
CHAPTER 5

Encouragement

Doing things a certain way, you put your

trust in God. -Moss Family

Trust in the Lord with all your heart, and do
not lean on your own understanding. In all
your ways acknowledge him, and he will
make straight your paths. Proverbs 3:5-6

CONNECTION

And we know that all things work together for good to them that love God, to them who are the called according to his purpose. Romans 8:28

We pulled up to the dream center childcare and realized that this was the SAME Church we visited the day before. We enrolled Lydia, so by August 28, she will be able to utilize this service. Until then, I have to pick her up and drop her off.

1.Read Matthew 1:18-25. What's the connection between God, Mary, and Joseph?

2. *Have you ever been sent to work doing one thing and then, years later, reflected, and you're so grateful you learned that skill set because now you're using it in a different way? If so, tell me about it.

3. Does this activate your Faith? What are you thinking?

Night 29  Seek

Reflect:

Memory verse: Proverbs 12:19
Create a index card with this scripture.
Carry this scripture with you for this week.
Recite this scripture twice a day minimum

WAIT

Day 30

Wait for the Lord; be strong and
take heart and wait for the Lord.
Psalm 27:14

Now that Lydia is taken care of, I focused on Elizabeth. In Florida, Pre-K has its own process. We completed all the paper work. So, we got her squared away, except there is a waitlist.

1. Read John 11:1-44 . Jot down what you've learned about waiting for God.

Night 30      # Seek

Reflect:

Prayer
Go lay hands on different places that God leads you to.
Go Pray for the sick and shut in
Go pray for your situation but for someone else
Don't sit home today, Go ,Walk, and Pray

WORSHIP

Worship the LORD with gladness; come before him with joyful songs. 3 Know that the LORD is God. It is he who made us, and we are his ; we are his people, the sheep of his pasture. 4 Enter his gates with thanksgiving and his courts with praise; give thanks to him and praise his name. Psalm 100:2-5

Worship night is a part of our morning routine as a household. Let's just say some days we get down longer than others. We sing and dance. God asked me to add this page JUST NOW. **Our song: "I got it" by Pastor Mike Jr, "Eagles" by Transformation Church, "Firm Foundation" Cody Canes, "I don't mind waiting" by Juanita Bynum, "Give me faith" by Elevation Church, "More than able" by Elevation Church, "See me through it "by Brandon Heath, "Another one" by Elevation Church, and "Fight on my knees" by Evan Craft**

1.What is worship?

2. How do you worship?

3. When do you worship?

Night 31  Seek

Reflect:

Worship for 30 min
Turn on worship music
display the words/lyrics on the screen
sing out loud
focus on God
eliminate distractions

TRUST

Trust in the Lord, and do good; dwell in the land and befriend faithfulness. Delight yourself in the Lord, and he will give you the desires of your heart. Commit your way to the Lord; trust in him, and he will act. Psalm 37:3-5

We went to ELC to see if we could enroll the children in a program that offers discounted childcare. The hiccup to qualify is that you have to be working. Well, it's a catch-22 because I want to work, but I need someone to watch my children so I can go for the interviews. The lady tells me to call a number, and this number will help us. We call Hope and receive a Navigator. She helped us with jobs, childcare, essentials, etc.

1. Who do you trust?

2. *If you don't trust anyone, I am curious to know what happened? Was it your childhood? Youth? Your adulthood? Come on, share with me so I can understand.

3. Are you a trustworthy person?

Night 32  # Seek

Reflect:

Prayer Walk
Get your water
Go walk and pray 20 min
Pray for whoever comes
to mind

HUMILITY

Day 33

Whatever you do, work at it with all your heart, as working for the Lord, not for human masters, 24 since you know that you will receive an inheritance from the Lord as a reward. It is the Lord Christ you are serving.
Colossians 3:23-24

> Husband got selected to go on an out-of-town job for a week. This was so exciting for our family. He has been working for two months and has received two certifications. I drove him to work that morning, and his car remained in the neighborhood for that week. His car needed an oil change.

1. How has favor been given to you in your life?

2. Do you remain humble or get arrogant because you were noticed?

3. *Read 1 Peter 5:5-11. What did you notice?

Night 33  **Seek**

Bible Plan
Download Bible App
Find a plan
Began the plan today

Reflect:

HELP

The Department of Children and Family told me the Navigator would call in a couple of days. I kid you not; later that day, the Navigator calls. She lets me explain where I am, and we put a plan into place. She reached out to a church and got us help with our tires. We were in need of getting two tires and an oil change.

1.When was the last time you asked someone for help? Who helped you?

2 After you received help, how did you feel? Now imagine if no one helped you, how do you think you would have went ? Praise him for providing or praise him in advance for what he will do.

3.*Watch Steps of Obedience by Demonay Moss on Youtube. What did you learn?

Night 34  # Seek

Reflect:

Worship for 1 Hour
Turn on worship music
display the words/lyrics on the screen
Sing out loud
Focus on God
Eliminate distractions
Read, Journal , Listen, Cry

Rest Day

1 Samuel 16. Draw a picture and Jot down what you learned

Sidenote I have ran into A LOT of stay at home moms. This was weird for me. I have always saw myself working and for me to be home for the past 4 months right now is crazy. I've been learning about running a business', franchising, writing book, creating journals, creating a course, virtual teaching, financial industry, debt free, investments, and building wealth while maintaining the house, caring and teaching my children at home.

Do you see yourself where you want to be? Where are you and where do you want to be? Do you believe God has you there on purpose for a purpose?

....

....

....

....

....

....

....

God of Also

CHAPTER 6

Encouragement
Doing things a certain way, God gives all things. -Moss Family

..... What, then, shall we say in response to these things? If God is for us, who can be against us? 32 He who did not spare his own Son, but gave him up for us all—how will he not also, along with him, graciously give us all things? Romans 8:28-32

....God also said to Moses, "Say to the Israelites, 'The Lord,[b] the God of your fathers—the God of Abraham, the God of Isaac and the God of Jacob—has sent me to you.'
"This is my name forever,
the name you shall call me
from generation to generation.
Exodus 3:13-15

STRONG

Day 36

Be strong and courageous. Do not be afraid or terrified because of them, for the Lord your God goes with you; he will never leave you nor forsake you."
Deuteronomy 31:6

Today, we got BUMPED. We were living in the one-bedroom for 1 day shy of 1 month. Getting bumped means someone has requested to live in the apartment we are in, so we have to move somewhere else. Mind you, Franklin is out of town until Friday, and we have three days to have everything packed and moved out by Friday.

1. When you feel the pressure of all your responsibilities, how do you respond?

2. *I thought being strong was for men. What do you think God meant when he called all of us to be strong and courageous (Joshua 1:9)? What does that look like for a woman?

3. Why do you think God had to remind us that he would never leave nor forsake us (Deuteronomy 31:6)?

Night 36      # Seek

Reflect:

Meditate
Deuteronomy 31
Proverbs 18

STRENGTH

Day 37

Honor and majesty surround him; strength and beauty fill his sanctuary. O nations of the world, recognize the Lord; recognize that the Lord is glorious and strong. Give to the Lord the glory he deserves! Bring your offering and come into his courts. Worship the Lord in all his holy splendor. Let all the earth tremble before him. Psalms 96: 6-9

So I began packing with Elizabeth, Landon, and Brooklynn on my chest. I began loading Franklin's car first. Oh yeah, Franklin's still out of town. I had to pack and load everything. Boxes fell off the kart, and the wind took some of our items away. We chased the items and got them back. I would stop and breathe in and out and remember God is with me while I am doing this. So when I got to the heavy boxes and I was loading them in the car, I would say "God help me 1, 2, 3", we would lift it together. I felt him helping me. Then within those three days, we were all loaded.

1. How did I help my family?

2. Based on the story you have learned about thus far, what can should we give God glory for?

3. Now it's your turn. What can you give God glory for?

Night 37  Seek

Reflect:

Now it's your turn
How have you helped your family this week? Surprise them if you haven't already.

LOST

Thomas said to him, "Lord, we don't know where you are going, so how can we know the way?" John 14:5

We had to find a place to go. We had options. We could move into another one-bedroom the same day we were asked to move out, or we could wait three days somewhere and move into a three-bedroom for the SAME price.

1. Have you ever felt lost? Not sure which is the right choice? Explain it.

2. What did you wind up choosing to do?

3. Reflecting back, what did God do to help you with the route you picked? What do you think he saved you from?

Night 38  # Seek

Reflect:

Memory verse: Psalm 37:23
Create a index card with this scripture.
Carry this scripture with you for this week.
Recite this scripture twice a day minimum

FAM

We decided to wait, so we went to a hotel suite for three days. My father-in-law and his wife helped us by covering half the hotel cost

1. When was the last time you helped one of your family members?

2. *Helping a family does not have to be financial. Remember in Series 1, when 10 of my family members came and helped us load things to Goodwill? How else could you help your family? I can help my family by _____.

3. Bear with each other and forgive one another if any of you has a grievance against someone. Forgive as the Lord forgave you (Colossians 3:13). Let's take some time to pray over your family. Find a quiet space, ensure no one is around, and verbally express how you feel after being asked about your family.

Night 39      Seek

Reflect:

Sermon
watch an online sermon.(pick wisely)
re-watch one of your pastor's sermons.
take notes
what is one take away you learned

SAY IT

Then he said to me, "Prophesy to these bones and say to them, 'Dry bones, hear the word of the Lord! Ezekiel 37: 4

There was a gap. We moved out of the neighborhood by 11 am, but we didn't get to move into the hotel suite until 3 pm. I took the kids to McDonald's to pass the time. Then I decided to go early and just ask because I had all these cold items in the car. I asked with all three of my children and explained that I had to pick up my fourth child at 3 pm, so I honestly needed to have my keys and food put away already. She asked, and they said "YES"!

1.Esther 4:6-17. What happened to Esther? Did she agree to go ASK?

2.In Esther, What did she want them to do to prepare before she boldly asked?

3.Ezekiel 37:1-14 This time God is directing Ezekiel to SAY It. What did God want him to say?

Night 40  # Seek

Reflect:

Prayer Journal
Ask God for what you need him to do for the people you know.
Ask God for what you need.
Ask God for what he wants from you.
After completing these exercises in this order, how do you feel? Remember, you can rip or keep.

CALCULATE

Day 41

For which of you, wanting to build a tower, doesn't first sit down and calculate the cost to see if he has enough to complete it? Luke 14:28

Before Franklin got back, I had already unloaded the bags we would need for those three nights, including refrigerator items. Food was ready. I picked up Lydia. Franklin arrived; he got dropped off in the old neighborhood by a coworker. We left the hotel and met them there. We both rode over to the hotel in our separate vehicles. We arrived at the hotel and rested.

1. How has me being at home instead of being at a brick and mortar helped my family?

2. How do you effectively manage your time for your lifestyle?

3. Take time to make a schedule, review your routine, or create a system so your household can run smoothly.

Night 41  **Seek**

Reflect:

Serve Ideas
Create sandwiches, Go pass them out
Go out and serve someone other than yourself
Pay for someone's meal
go on a lunch date with a friend and buy their meal
Serve your family

Rest Day

Over this past week, reflect, how has God spoken to you? What's one thing your going to change?

GOD OF ABRAHAM

CHAPTER 7

Encouragement
Doing things a certain way you
experience the God of Abram.
-Moss Family

After this, the word of the Lord came to Abram in a vision:

"Do not be afraid, Abram. I am your shield, your very great reward.
[b]"Genesis 15:1

ALSO

For thus says the Lord God, "Behold, I Myself will search for My sheep and seek them out. Ezekiel 34:11

Sunday, we were invited to visit Oasis Church. This was the Church that helped us with the 4 brand-new tires and an oil change. When we were about to leave, they asked us to step into the conference room, and they began to ask, "What ELSE do you all need?" They helped us bag meat, provided two gift cards to Old Navy (for Lydia's uniform and shoes), clothes for the kids, and two gift cards to eat out. We thank God for Hope; she connected us with them.

1.Read 1 Kings 3:10-15. Solomon asked for wisdom, but what ELSE did God give him?

2.Do you believe God will give you more than you ask for? Has this ever happened to you before?

3.Do you have a home church? Why or why not?

Night 43　　 # Seek

Reflect:

PROVIDE

"Your Father knows what you need before you ask him." Matthew 6:8

We hadn't gotten Franklin's car an oil change yet, so he was hesitant to drive it to work. The Church provided us with an Uber gift card for him to go back and forth to work so he wouldn't have to take a chance on getting stranded. They knew the only reason we had to move it out of the neighborhood was that they would tow it.

1.Read Genesis 22:1-15 (What did God provide?)

2.Read John 8:1-11 (What did God provide?)

3.Read Judges 13: 2-5 (What did God provide?)

Night 44  # Seek
Reflect:

Journaling: Proverbs 22:17
write out how you feel
write about the scriptures
your focusing on

REDO

Day 45

So we rebuilt the wall till all of it reached half its height, for the people worked with all their heart.
Nehemiah 4: 6

Now, it's Monday morning, and Franklin's off to work. I reloaded the van with all of our stuff from the suite by 11 am. But I don't get the keys until 4 pm. I took the kids to the park. Then I picked Lydia up, and I took the kids back to the park. Then we headed to get the keys. This time the Church had two families meet us at our house. They helped watch all the kids, and they helped me unload the van to our next landing unit.

1.Read Nehemiah 4:14 (How were they encouraged?)

2.Chronicles 16:9 (What kind of support does God offer us?)

3.Read Ezekiel 36:25 (What did you learn about the word "clean"?

Night 45  # Seek

Reflect:

Tidy Up
I know you have a lot on your plate. Humbly, where do you think you can use 5 minutes to tidy up each day in your schedule? Whether that's in your car, mailbox, home, phone storage, computer storage, work, or elsewhere

SING

Day 46

Sing to God, you kingdoms of
the earth, sing praise to the
Lord, Psalm 68:32

September 2, we got to experience our first encounter at the beach. We've been in FL for 3 months. We loved it so much that once a week, we started going. On Saturdays from 4-8, there is worship on the water. I got to sing LIVE on the microphone. The beach is ONLY 9 minutes away from us, and it's FREE.

1.Do you think God cares how you sound when you sing to him?

2.What song has been on your heart lately? Do you sing them out loud?

3.*Read Psalm 119:164-166. What does it say about praising him?

Night 46      # Seek

Reflect:

Praise Him
Does the song you're thinking about please God? I dare you to sing praises out loud throughout this week to please God.

REMEMBER

Day 47
As iron sharpens iron,
so one person sharpens another
Proverbs 27:17

Last night, God protected us. We walked to the park close to dark, played, and had a great time. A boat came up to the Riverwalk Park and handed out glow-in-the-dark bracelets for all the children. While we were there, a lady who remembered us from the museum she had stopped in front of me and said, "You have beautiful eyes", she recognized us. Her daughter was playing with my son, and she said, "I thought that was you." We began to talk about raising children and adjusting to having a newborn. It was such a great conversation.

1.1 Peter 4:8-10 What is God reminding you?

2.1 Thessalonians 5:11 How did the woman encourage me? How did her stopping that day help for the next day?

3.1 Samuel 18:1-5 What did you notice about David and Jonathan's friendship?

Night 47  # Seek Share:

Sermon
watch an online sermon.(pick wisely)
re-watch one of your pastor's
sermons.
take notes
what is one take away you learned

AUTHORITY

The thief comes only to steal and kill and destroy; God have come that they may have life, and have it to the full. John 10:10

The enemy attacked my husband. While he was sleepwalking, he messed up something. I was aware, and when we returned from the park, I prayed for my family and cast evil spirits out of my home. I said, "This is God's house; enemy, you must flee." Knowing hubby is under attack, everything he is saying while he sleeps, I am saying "Jesus." When he woke up, he realized what happened, he prayed, and he fixed what was messed up. I thank God for protecting my husband and not allowing the enemy to dominate his future. I encouraged him and told him how proud I was of him for cleaning up his mess and how he took initiative, made bottle, and fed Brooklynn.

1.Matthew 4:1-11 Who led Jesus to be tempted by the spirit?

2.Philippians 2:9-11 Whose name has the authority to make every knee bow?

3.Do you notice someone in your life who isn't acting normal? I encourage you not to entertain that spirit by arguing with it. Instead, PRAY and call on His NAME.

Night 48  **Seek** Share:

Prayer
Who in your life needs prayer
Pray for others
Write a prayer out for 3 people

Rest Day

Day 49

Read John 14. Draw a picture and jot down what you learned

....

....

....

....

....

....

....

....

....

....

....

GOD OF MIRACLES

CHAPTER 8

Encouragement
Doing things a certain way you will see the miracles of God. -Moss Family

11 God did extraordinary miracles through Paul, 12 so that even handkerchiefs and aprons that had touched him were taken to the sick, and their illnesses were cured and the evil spirits left them. Acts 19:11-12

INTEREST

Today, the lady in the neighborhood with two daughters who go to my children's school, Brandy, took my children to school. She asked me, and I said YES! After dropping the kids off, she gave me kid uniforms. Now both children have school uniforms. Since school started a month ago, they had two uniforms, and we would wash and repeat. Praise God for providing even though we didn't ask. Thank God for knowing what we need.

Philippians 2:4 What does this mean to you?

Luke 6:30 & Hebrews 13:16: What pleases God?

Tell me about two experiences you've had.

1. How has someone helped you, and they didn't expect anything in return?

2. How have you helped someone and didn't expect anything in return?

Night 50  **Seek** Share:

Goals
jot down your goals.
find scriptures that will help you achieve your goal
recite your goals minimum of two times a day

DATE NIGHT

Day 51

But someone will say, "You have faith and I have works." Show me your faith apart from your works, and I will show you my faith by my works. James 2:18

Today the school just emailed us about Parent Night Out at the local Church. I contacted Franklin to see if he was interested. He said yes! I enrolled all four children. Look at that; we have childcare for three hours! We have two gift cards left from Series 1 when that church community blessed us. We were saving it for date night and BAM.

1.Colossians 4:3 How did Paul humble himself? What was his prayer?

2.Take advantage of the opportunities presented to you. Through prayer, make a decision. It could change your future. List the opportunities you have been offered.

3.What has been troubling you concerning making a decision?

Night 51  Seek Share:

Meditate
Psalm 79
Psalm 145
Exodus 34

BIRDS

Day 52

Therefore encourage one
another and build one
another up, just as you are
doing 1 Thessalonians 5:11

At the women's conference, I met Arianna. She is married and has a son. They are fairly new to Florida as well. So I invited her out to parents' night out, which is a free program where the Church watches your child for three hours while you get to go on a date away from the child, and they provide dinner. We take our children, and we enjoy the gift card date night experience.

1. Read Matthew 6:25-34. Draw what comes to mind.

12. Invite a friend or couple to join you for lunch on Sunday after Church.

3. Read John 15:1-8. What are Jesus' commands?

Night 52    **Seek**   Share:

Sermon
Watch an online sermon.(pick wisely)
Re-watch one of your pastor's sermons.
Take notes
What is one take away you learned

OBSTACLE

And it will be said, "Build up, build up, prepare the way, Remove every obstacle out of the way of My people."
Isaiah 57:14

God provided someone to bless us with $20 for gas. We went to a gas station. Brooklynn, Landon, and I walked into the store. The owner was there, and he offered Landon a lollipop. He took it. We walked out, and I said, "Landon did you say thank you?" Landon said, "No, can we go back inside?" and I said, "Yes," mind you I am crying because I'm vulnerable. I just get so excited about what and how God does miracles all in one day for everyone. Landon goes back inside and says "Thank you." The owner says, "You're welcome, here is another lollipop for thanking me." Landon was shocked and said, "Now, I can give this to my sisters!"

1.When faced with an obstacle, what is normally the first thing you do?

2.Ephesians 4:32 How can you be kind today?

3..Deuteronomy 15:6 This week God will bless you, jot down when he does, and tell a friend what he did for you. Be intentionally on the lookout as you seek him.

Night 53      # Seek   Share:

Bible Plan
Download Bible App
Find a plan
Began the plan
today

REJOICE

Day 54

Rejoice in the Lord always;
again I will say, rejoice.
Philippians 4:4

September 21, 2023, I dropped Landon off at Head Start daycare; it was his first day, so the girls had to come. Then, I dropped the girls off at school. Brooklynn and I went home. Date night with hubby is this Friday, so I did my hair, found my outfit, and made sure I was well-groomed.

1. I can remember when I was at home with both kids, and now look. Do you remember when you asked God for something, then looking back you see how he worked it out?

2. Why is it important to prepare?

3. Personal Reflection: create a T-chart: How do you prepare for a date vs How do you prepare to spend time with God

---

Night 54  **Seek**   Share:

Worship for 30 min
Turn on worship music
display the words/lyrics on the screen
sing out loud
focus on God
eliminate distractions

TIMING

Day 55

For everything there is a season, and a
time for every matter under heaven.

Ecclesiastes 3:1

September 21, 2023, I applied that night, and this morning, I got called for an interview while preparing for date night. Remember today was Landon's first day at Headstart Childcare. The interview was at 2 pm. Landon gets picked up at 2:45 pm. I left the interview fast, and I made it just in time to get Landon. I did well in the interview.

Thursday, 9/21, I had my first interview in Bradenton. Mon, 9/25, I got hired. Next Mon, 10/2, I started my first day of work. I have 17 students. Praise God. The first day, I was thrown into my class, and I got to run it with God's lead guidance.

1. The interview wasn't part of my routine today. Did you notice I squeezed it in? How do you act when plans suddenly change?

2. What if I told you that sometimes God can change your situation in seconds if you change your plans? Do you believe me? Have you ever witnessed this done before in your life or someone else's?

3. Read Isaiah 55:8-9. Jot down what you think.

Night 55  # Seek   Share:

Meditate
Ecclesiatics 3
Proverbs 16:9
2 Peter 3:8

Sketch

Read Esther 5. Read and Draw what comes to mind

....

....

....

....

....

....

....

....

....

....

GOD'S FAMILY

CHAPTER 9

Encouragement
God loves you! -Moss Family

19 So now you Gentiles are no longer strangers and foreigners. You are citizens along with all of God's holy people. You are members of God's family. **20** Together, we are his house, built on the foundation of the apostles and the prophets. And the cornerstone is Christ Jesus himself. Ephesians 2:19-20

FAVOR

> September 21, 2023, Same day, I checked with stay-at-home Bandi LAST MINUTE. Bandi is a lady I met in the Airbnb neighborhood; her daughters attend the same school as my girls. She agreed to watch Brooklynn for me so I could make it to my interview. While Landon was at Headstart and the girls were at school, Hubby was at work. I went to the interview. After the interview, Bandi kept saying, "you're fine, go ahead and pamper yourself today. I will watch her." I agreed.

1.Read Matthew 7:7-12 What are we called to do?

2.Read Mark 9:23: What's possible if you believe?

3.Read John 14:13-14 How does God feel about us asking and accepting help?

Night 57  # Seek Share:

Rest in God
Have your time with God,
How ever you need to!

REPEAT

Here are two quotes from our children when we asked "What do we always do?" "Mommy and Daddy pray to God together with us at bedtime every night and they read the bible day and night." the kids said. "Now, we pay off debt so we can go on the Dave Ramsey Show and screams "I want to be debt free!" the kids said

1.What routines do you have with your children?

2.How would your children describe your relationship with God?

3.Psalm 127:3 (What does God say about his children?

Night 58  # Seek   Share:

Prayer Journal
Think of the children in your life write a paper for 3 children

CHILDREN

Day 59

The Lord bless you and keep you; the Lord make his face shine on you and be gracious to you; the Lord turn his face toward you and give you peace.
Numbers 6:24-26

9/22/23 We picked the kids up from childcare at the Church, and they gave all parents containers of mac n cheese and sausages for each child. We were thrilled. We took the children to the other Church so we could have 3 hours for DATE NIGHT while they watched and fed the kids dinner. Our first date but not the last date night of 2023. We had so much fun. We came and picked them up. They told us every 4 months they offer this service so follow them on Facebook. On our way out they gave us a box of cheese pizza to take home.

Study---Matthew 19:26, Luke 18:16, Mark 9:37

write a prayer:

Night 59  **Seek** Share:

Sermon
Watch an online sermon or go (pick wisely)
Sermons. (children)
Take Notes
What is one take away you learned?

DATE NIGT TOO

Let's talk about DATE NIGHT 9/22/23. What a great time we had. It was full of laughter, conversation, and silence. We did not have any expectations of what the night would be, so it created intimacy. We went to Outback Steakhouse again (without our kids), and we loved the atmosphere. Everything was amazing. We used our gift card we received the day of our wedding anniversary (August 8). I think I smiled the WHOLE night. (never happened the WHOLE night before on our old dates.) I just want to give my husband and God props for this day. After dinner, my hubby even opened the car door for me. (that used to be his normal, so it's coming back. YES!!!

1.Read Genesis 2:18, what is God revealing to you?

2.Proverbs 18:22, What is God revealing to you?

3.1 Peter 4:8, What is God calling us to do?

Night 60      Seek   Share:

Bible Plan
Download Bible App
Find a plan
Began the plan today

HOSPITALITY

Day 61
Do not neglect to show hospitality to strangers, for by this some have entertained angels without knowing it.
Hebrew 13:2

What a day! Today, the apartment complex invited us to the pool. We swam for 3 hours. We didn't know people noticed we lived here, let alone that we moved. They asked what happened to us (you remember in series 1, we lived in a 1-bedroom). Both apartments are in the same neighborhood. We met many different people. My son became comfortable with the water because one of the elderly men took him by his side and respected his boundaries. Also, the complex provided food; they had sandwiches and fruit.

1..When was the last time you were shown hospitality?

2.When was the last time you gave hospitality?

3.When was the last time God has shown you or others around you hospitality?

Night 61  Seek Share:

Friendship
Choose a scripture that has been on your mind
Contact your friend and share
Listen to your friend thoughts. Then share what you learned

AVAILABLE

A friend loves at all times, and a brother is born for adversity.
Proverbs 17:17

We found out that Monday night, the Church provided childcare on community group nights. So Mondays, my hubby and I would meet at home, then we would all get in one car and drive to Bible study. Today was our first visit, and we met two cool married couples!

1.Are you available to attend a small group?

2.What are your pros and cons about being involved in a community group?

3.Do you value friendships? why or why not?

Night 62  Seek Share:

Meditate
Hebrews 10:24-25, Ephesians 4:15-16, Acts 2:42-47
Discover what God says about being around others.

MULTITASKING

Day 63

My son, do not despise the Lord's
discipline or be weary of his reproof, for
the Lord reproves him whom he loves,
as a father the son in whom he delights.
Proverbs 3:11-12

Franklin has been cleaning, tending to kids, making plates, cleaning dishes, doing laundry, sweeping, and spending less time drinking. I am so thankful that the Holy Spirit entered. If you didn't know, Conviction is REAL. Prayer changes things.

1. 2 Samuel 11: Describe Uriah's character.

2. 1 Samuel: Describe Elkanah's character.

Night 63  **Seek** Share:

Describe
Describe the men in your life.
How did they treat you?
How are they treating you now?
How do you view the trinity (God, Holy Spirit, and Son)?

Rest Day

HOW I SPEND TIME WITH GOD

Tip 2 in the bible

Normally, I find a quiet place.
Gather all material
Pray/Read
Draw/Journal/Color
Listen/Write
Most days I can get 30 min in Morning before kids wake up
Most days I can get 30min in Evening when kids are asleep

What's your routine?

SOAK IN GOD

CHAPTER 10

As soon as I heard these words I sat down and wept and mourned for days, and I continued fasting and praying before the God of heaven. Nehemiah 1:4

Fasting/Praying

I am so proud of you, You made it, this far. God has something special for you. This next Chapter is dedicated to you and it's from Vol. 1. Let's spend this next two weeks Soaking in God's word through prayer and fasting. Spend Time reflecting on all God has done and is doing and will do in your life.

PLAN

How long will you fast?
What are your rules for this fast?
some examples: (no sweets, no TV, no social media, fruit and veggie, water only etc) List your rules below.

Why are you fasting? What are you fasting for? Example. Get closer to God, my marriage, transition etc) List your rules below.

Soak

Read Judge 15. Jot down every thing that stood out to you.

....

....

....

....

....

....

....

....

....

....

....

....

....

....

....

Soak

Read Judge 14 . Jot down every thing that stood out to you.

....

....

....

....

....

....

....

....

....

....

....

....

....

....

....

....

....

Soak

Day 2

Read Mark 5: 1-20 . Jot down every thing that stood out to you.

....

....

....

....

....

....

....

....

....

....

....

....

....

....

....

....

....

....

Soak

Read Deuteronomy 5 . Jot down every thing that stood out to you.

....

....

....

....

....

....

....

....

....

....

....

....

....

....

....

....

Soak

Day 3

Read Exodus 2 . Jot down every thing that stood out to you.

....

....

....

....

....

....

....

....

....

....

....

....

....

....

....

....

Soak

Read Nehemiah 4 . Jot down every thing that stood out to you.

....

....

....

....

....

....

....

....

....

....

....

....

....

....

....

....

....

Soak

Read Colossians 4 . Jot down every thing that stood out to you.

....

....

....

....

....

....

....

....

....

....

....

....

....

....

....

....

Soak

Read Song of Songs 6 . Jot down every thing that stood out to you.

Soak

Read John 3 . Jot down every thing that stood out to you.

··

··

··

··

··

··

··

··

··

··

··

··

··

··

··

··

Soak

Read Genesis 28 . Jot down every thing that stood out to you.

....

....

....

....

....

....

....

....

....

....

....

....

....

....

....

Soak

Read Galatians 3 . Jot down every thing that stood out to you.

....

....

....

....

....

....

....

....

....

....

....

....

....

....

....

....

Soak

Read Psalm 46 . Jot down every thing that stood out to you.

....

....

....

....

....

....

....

....

....

....

....

....

....

....

....

....

Soak

Read Matthew 7-15 . Jot down every thing that stood out to you.

....

....

....

....

....

....

....

....

....

....

....

....

....

....

....

....

Soak

Read Joshua 1. Jot down every thing that stood out to you.

Soak

Read Philippians 4. Jot down every thing that stood out to you.

....

....

....

....

....

....

....

....

....

....

....

....

....

....

....

....

Soak

Read Psalm 55 . Jot down every thing that stood out to you.

....

....

....

....

....

....

....

....

....

....

....

....

....

....

....

....

....

Soak

Read 1 King 19 . Jot down every thing that stood out to you.

··

··

··

··

··

··

··

··

··

··

··

··

··

··

··

··

Soak

Read 2 Timothy 3 . Jot down every thing that stood out to you.

....

....

....

....

....

....

....

....

....

....

....

....

....

....

....

....

Soak

Read Psalms 119 . Jot down every thing that stood out to you.

....

....

....

....

....

....

....

....

....

....

....

....

....

....

....

....

....

Soak

Read Ecclesiastes 1. Jot down every thing that stood out to you.

....

....

....

....

....

....

....

....

....

....

....

....

....

....

....

....

Soak

Read Genesis 6-10 . Jot down every thing that stood out to you.

....

....

....

....

....

....

....

....

....

....

....

....

....

....

....

....

Soak

Read Hebrew 1. Jot down every thing that stood out to you.

....

....

....

....

....

....

....

....

....

....

....

....

....

....

....

....

REFLECTIONS

Name:

Date:

HOW HAS THIS FASTED HELPED YOU?

CHALLENGES OVERCOME
• Reflect on the challenges faced and how they were overcome.

THINGS I'M GRATEFUL FOR
• Write a list to acknowledge what you're thankful for.

GOALS FOR THIS YEAR
• Set a few important goals for this upcoming week.

PERSONAL DEVELOPMENT
• Reflect on personal growth and areas for improvement.

RELATIONSHIPS
• Set goals related to family, friends, or social life.

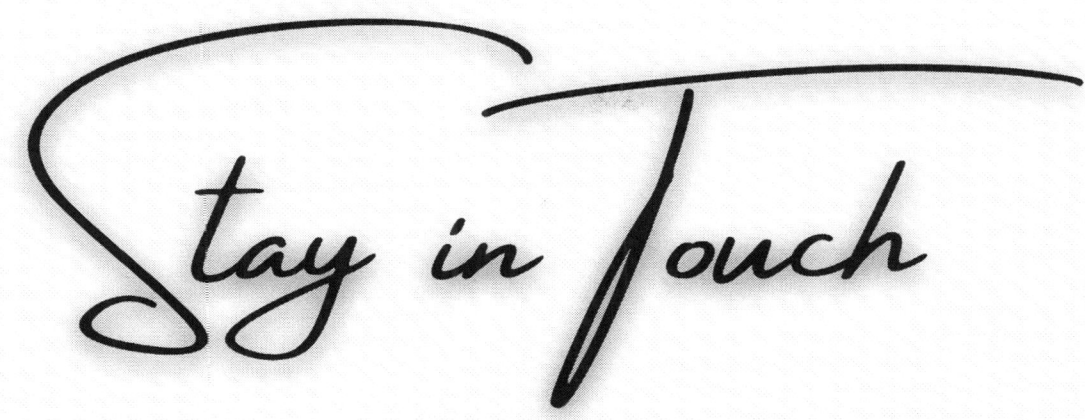

<u>Stay Connected</u>

Sticky bible study is a safe place to learn how to grow in your relationship with God. Live Bible Studies and Book Studies.

@stickybiblestudy

Get Freebies, Join our email list MAILCHIMP

Changebydee is a platform to help you learn and become debt free through Godly principles.

@changebydee

https://www.youtube.com/@demonaymoss

Register for Freebie!

Made in the USA
Middletown, DE
29 November 2025

23534592R00057